For the Love of Mr. Max

by Barbara Ann Simone
Illustrated by Sarah Pecorino

Copyright © 2014 Kids' Grief Relief

All rights reserved. No part of this book may be used or reproduced by any means, graphic, electronic, or mechanical, including photocopying, recording, taping, or by any information storage retrieval system without the written permission of the author except in the case of brief quotations embodied in critical articles and reviews.

ISBN: 978-0-9856334-8-6
(softcover book)

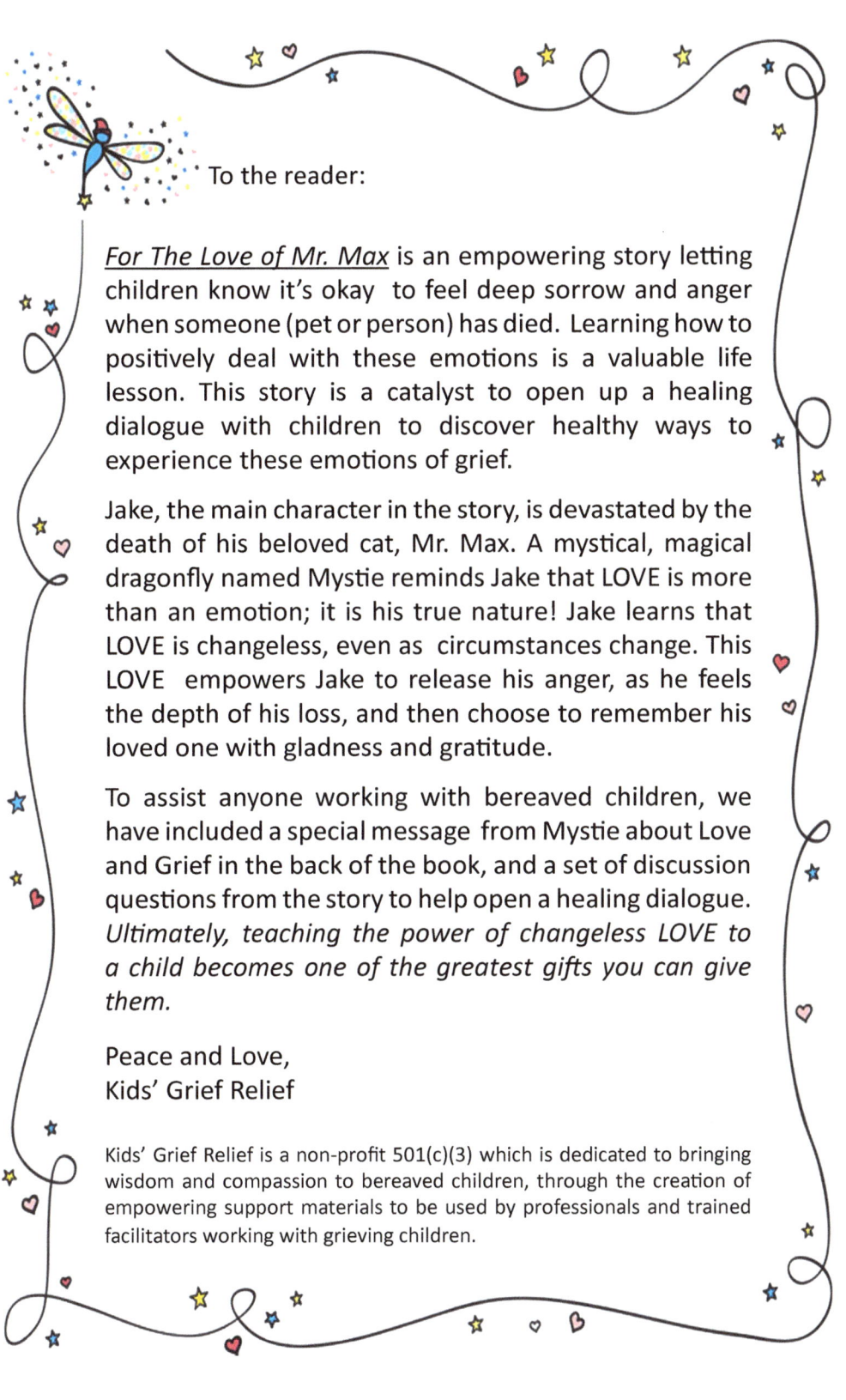

To the reader:

For The Love of Mr. Max is an empowering story letting children know it's okay to feel deep sorrow and anger when someone (pet or person) has died. Learning how to positively deal with these emotions is a valuable life lesson. This story is a catalyst to open up a healing dialogue with children to discover healthy ways to experience these emotions of grief.

Jake, the main character in the story, is devastated by the death of his beloved cat, Mr. Max. A mystical, magical dragonfly named Mystie reminds Jake that LOVE is more than an emotion; it is his true nature! Jake learns that LOVE is changeless, even as circumstances change. This LOVE empowers Jake to release his anger, as he feels the depth of his loss, and then choose to remember his loved one with gladness and gratitude.

To assist anyone working with bereaved children, we have included a special message from Mystie about Love and Grief in the back of the book, and a set of discussion questions from the story to help open a healing dialogue. *Ultimately, teaching the power of changeless LOVE to a child becomes one of the greatest gifts you can give them.*

Peace and Love,
Kids' Grief Relief

Kids' Grief Relief is a non-profit 501(c)(3) which is dedicated to bringing wisdom and compassion to bereaved children, through the creation of empowering support materials to be used by professionals and trained facilitators working with grieving children.

CHAPTER ONE

MAX

I can't remember a time when Mr. Max wasn't a part of my life. My mom has a picture of me when I first started to walk. Mr. Max is right next to me. It looks like he's trying to help me stand up straight, because he's rubbing his orange and white body next to my small, chubby leg. The picture sits on our mantle where everyone can see it.

I like that picture.

My name is Jake and I'm eleven years old. I like photography, music, video games, and animals, especially my special cat Mr. Max.

I remember Mr. Max at every birthday party, holiday celebration, picnic, you name it. The only time he wasn't home with me was when we went on vacation. He went to a place called "The Cats Only Inn," where he got great care. I was never happy to leave him there, but the people who worked there were always glad to see him.

I believed he was my cat, though my mom, in a teasing voice, would remind me that he was her cat. After all, she would say, Mr. Max chose HER four years before I was born!

She never thought about owning a cat. Then one day a small orange and white kitten appeared in her front yard. The shy kitten slowly walked up to her when she called it. I don't know if it was "love at first sight", but I do know the moment she picked him up, he had found a permanent home.

At first she just called him Max, but as he grew, she changed it to Mr. Max because there was something regal about him. Maybe it was the way he was so neat and tidy about his litter box. Maybe it was the way he looked at people with curious interest. He listened to everyone's conversation as if he understood every word that was spoken. I know he understood everything about me.

So, I think Mr. Max was clear about what happened when I was two years old. My mom and dad got divorced. My dad moved far away and I stayed with my mom and Mr. Max. That's when Mr. Max started sleeping with me. Before the divorce, he slept with my mom and dad. Since the divorce, he has slept with me.

My mom re-married three years ago. I have a wonderful new step-dad, but Mr. Max still sleeps with me. Mr. Max was my buddy, and I thought of him as my furry brother, who purred a lot.

I remember my mom telling my new step-dad that Mr. Max was part of our family, and he would have the opportunity to learn how much fun our cat was.

My step-dad learned fast. Whenever he brought a surprise to me, he would have a new toy for Mr. Max. Our home had a lot of cat toys, and we all enjoyed playing with Mr. Max.

CHAPTER TWO

GINGER

My friend Sarah has the coolest dog named Victor. He's a black lab who catches a Frisbee better than any dog I've ever seen in person or on TV.

When I asked my parents about getting a dog like Victor, I was told I had to be a bit older. They suggested I get a different type of pet.

We all went to the pet store, where I discovered how neat guinea pigs are! They're soft, cute and noisy! They whistle and grunt when they're excited. A happy guinea pig can do something called popcorning. When it's very happy, it jumps straight up in the air!

I knew owning a guinea pig would be different than owning a dog, yet I immediately wanted one. My mom asked the pet store owner if guinea pigs got along with cats.

"Some cats get along with guinea pigs", we were told.

I knew Mr. Max would be fine with a guinea pig. He was wise enough to know that if I liked one, it had to be okay. So I chose one, and named her Ginger.

Once Ginger was in our home, she made the craziest, silliest sounds! I liked picking her up and she liked being held by me. I knew she would enjoy being part of our family.

I put her cage on the floor, between my bed and my desk. Mr. Max noticed Ginger, but he acted as normal as usual. Ginger didn't mind Mr. Max walking around my room, and Mr. Max didn't mind sharing me with her. Everyone got along just fine.

I quickly learned how to take good care of Ginger. I fed her special pellet food, with hay and vegetables. I cleaned her cage out every day, and provided her with fresh water. Guinea pigs thrive on human conversation, so I made it a point to talk to her whenever I was in my room. She heard a lot of stuff about my life! I loved to watch her play with her toys and run on her wheel, as she made her unique guinea pig noises!

There was one thing that I didn't say a word about. I noticed Mr. Max was moving a lot slower lately. Instead of leaping and prancing all over my desk and shelves, he crept slowly around my room and slept more. I figured he was just getting older, but I didn't want to say anything, not even to Ginger.

I bet she knew anyway.

CHAPTER THREE

NO WAY!

One horrible day my life changed forever. I got off the school bus around 3:15, and saw my step-dad's car in the driveway. That was unusual. He always came around 6:30, right before we had dinner.

I opened the door, shocked at what I saw. On the couch was my sobbing mom with my step-dad sitting next to her. He looked very upset, too.

"What's going on?' I asked in a trembling voice.

"Mr. Max is gone", my step-dad said sadly.

"What do you mean gone? Did he run away or something?"

"He had a stroke this morning. Your mother called me. I came home from work and we took Mr. Max to Dr. G."

"What did Dr. G do?"

My mother stopped crying. She looked right at me and took a deep breath.

Gently she said, "He euthanized Mr. Max. That means he gave him some drugs to put him to sleep, so he could die peacefully. The stroke had made him very, very sick."

I was trying to put all the words she said in some sort of order, so they could make sense, but I couldn't.

"But why did he have to die? If he was sick, Dr. G should have made him better!"

"Jake, Mr. Max couldn't walk or move by himself anymore. He couldn't focus his eyes to look anywhere, or hold his neck up. His life as a cat was gone." The tears were flowing steadily down my mom's face.

My head started hurting so much that I wanted to close my eyes and pretend I didn't hear what my mom had just said. My stomach ached. I felt I was going to vomit.

"If he was so sick, how did he take the medicine from Dr. G?"

"Dr. G put medicine in a needle, and gave him some shots. Mr. Max was never in any pain. We were with him the entire time."

My mind was racing with all sad images of what my mom just told me. I felt my knees wobble a bit, so I sat down on the floor.

Wh..wh…where is his body?

 We put his body in a wooden box and buried him under the red maple tree outside, next to the house." We thought it best that you didn't have to see any of what happened."

"But he was my cat too! This is horrible! This can't be real!"

I somehow got my strength back to stand up. Frantically, I ran outside to take a look.

There, under the red maple was a statue of our garden angel, in a new position. Either my mom or step-dad had written "Mr. Max" on it. The ground had been recently dug up, as there were some piles of dirt around the edges of the statue.

I stared at the grave in disbelief. I couldn't read the letters anymore because I was crying so much. My beloved Mr. Max was dead and there was nothing I could do about it. I felt helpless and confused.

For a brief moment I saw a blue dragonfly with a yellow star on its tail, hovering over the grave. The dragonfly started flying in circles all around the garden angel.

I wiped some tears away to see clearer, but it seemed to have disappeared.

Wildly, I ran back inside.

"I can't believe you did all of this WITHOUT ME! Mr. Max was like a brother to me! How could you both be so mean?" I screamed in anger.

"It was a very hard thing to do. Thank goodness Dr. G. was so compassionate. He puts many pets to sleep so they can die peacefully." said my step-dad.

"But I never got a chance to say good-by to him. I didn't get a chance to pet him for the last time! THIS ISN'T FAIR!"

I ran upstairs to my room and slammed the door shut. I buried my head in my pillow and yelled and cried. I was shocked that Mr. Max was gone. Forever…

CHAPTER FOUR

ANGER

From upstairs I heard my mom and step-dad talking over what had happened. They were shaken up about Mr. Max and double-guessing whether or not they should have gotten me from school to see the whole thing. It felt like everything in my home was upside-down.

I was angry at my mom for thinking I wasn't old enough to handle what happened to Mr. Max. I was mad at my step-dad for burying Mr. Max without my help. I think I was even mad at Mr. Max for having a stroke when I wasn't home. This was confusing to me because I loved him so much.

"This is the worst thing that ever happened to me," I shouted to Ginger, who was staring at me like I was someone she didn't know. "I feel like I am going to be upset forever."

Then I saw the same blue dragonfly with the yellow star on its tail, hovering over Ginger's cage. It flew inside, right up to her. I had the feeling the dragonfly was talking to Ginger. Ginger was making noises back to the dragonfly.

"Who are you?" I demanded.

"My name is Mystie. *What's Dragon-You-Down?*"

"You know what's "dragon-me-down", you dumb dragonfly!

You saw Mr. Max's grave! You know he's dead!

And my parents kept me away from the whole thing!

Get lost ! I don't want you around me or Ginger!"

The blue dragonfly disappeared.

14

CHAPTER FIVE

ANGER IS AS ANGER DOES

I felt angry all week.

Mr. Max died on Monday, yet by Thursday I was still feeling really mad and upset. I barely spoke to my parents.

At school, I was completely distracted. One of my teachers asked me if something was bothering me, and I said something about a headache. I told him I was sure I would be better in a few days. I wondered if he believed me, because I didn't believe me.

I couldn't focus.

The only thoughts running through my mind were:

- *My parents are really mean!*

- *Mr. Max would have wanted me there when he was put to sleep!*

- *I am old enough to handle what Dr. G did!*

- *Mr. Max should have waited till I came home from school to have a stroke!*

- *My room feels all wrong without him.*

- *I hate this whole thing!*

- *It's not fair!*

When my friends asked me what was wrong, I just shrugged them off. I didn't feel like talking to anyone about anything.

After school each day, I played video games. It felt awful not having Mr. Max sit with me. He was my greatest cheerleader, even though sometimes he would walk across the screen at the absolute worst time! He purred extra loud when I went up a level in a game. Now I didn't even care about my score.

One night my mom made my favorite dinner of beef tacos with all the extras. I barely finished my meal, and didn't even have seconds, which is rare for me. I just wasn't very hungry. My whole body felt wrong. It was hard to sleep. I missed Mr. Max so-o-o much.

My parents tried to talk to me and tell me they were sorry about the whole thing, but I wouldn't listen.

And for those days that I was so "busy" being mad and sad, I forgot about Ginger. I forgot that someone in my family was counting on my love to take care of her.

CHAPTER SIX

BIG TROUBLE

As I was sitting in Math class on Thursday afternoon, my principal walked into the classroom. Quietly, she whispered something to my teacher. The next thing I knew, I was invited to the principal's office.

As I walked down the hall with the principal, I was trying to come up with a story to explain why my grades had gone down during the week. I was sure that's why she wanted to talk to me in private. As we got close to the office, I was surprised to see my mom standing in the hallway. She looked very upset. She looked me right in the eyes with a strange look, like she wanted to cry, but was trying not to

"I came to pick you up. We have to go right away to see Dr. G. Your step-father is there right now with Ginger."

From the moment I heard her say "Ginger", I felt a pang in my chest. I didn't hear another word after that. I felt a bolt of lightning hit me with a shocking fact.

I had forgotten to take care of my sweet guinea pig all week!

I sprinted wildly to the car, with my mom walking quickly behind me. As we drove to Dr. G's office, neither of us said a word. We were both extremely upset.

My mind was racing with a zillion thoughts about what could be happening to Ginger:

How sick is she?　　　　*What if she dies?*

What if she has to be euthanized like Mr. Max?

I felt scared and terrified about what I would find at the vet.

When we finally got to Dr. G's office, I ran in ahead of my mom. In one of the smaller examination rooms, I saw Dr. G holding Ginger. He was talking to my step-dad. I rushed into the room with a frantic look on my face.

"It's okay Jake", said Dr. G in a calming voice. "Your guinea pig gave us a scare. She'll be okay. I gave her a shot to help her feel better. What happened this week?"

I looked at my step-dad who evidently knew what happened. "It's okay Jake", he said calmly.

I started petting Ginger. I couldn't look DR. G in the eyes.

Sheepishly I muttered, "I forgot to take care of her."

DR. G. placed Ginger in my arms. He put his hand on my shoulder.

"I bet you've been upset about Mr. Max. It's hard to let go of someone you love. He was a special member of your family and I am sorry for your loss, Jake. Mr. Max had a great life with you and your family. I never like having to euthanize a family pet, yet it's part of being a veterinarian."

I wanted to say something to Dr. G, but my mind went blank. Dr. G. smiled down at Ginger and started petting her. "I know you won't let this happen to Ginger again. Right Jake?"

"Ye...yes… sir", I stammered. I was shaking when I spoke.

"I promise to take care of Ginger **every** day."

CHAPTER SEVEN

MYSTIE

On the way home, I sat in the back seat with Ginger next to me in her cage. I didn't feel angry anymore. I felt relieved because Ginger was going to be okay. But I didn't feel okay about what I did, or rather, what I didn't do. How could I love Ginger so much, but forget to take care of her? I was confused, upset, and sad.

My mom turned from the front seat to look at Ginger. She smiled. She told me something unusual had happened, which helped her discover Ginger was sick. She was making herself a cup of tea, when she saw a small, bluish colored insect flying around the house. She followed it upstairs to Ginger's cage, where the flying insect seemed to disappear. That's when she saw Ginger lying down in the corner of the cage, breathing heavily. Immediately she called my step dad, who came home from work to take Ginger to the vet.

I was just about to ask her what happened to the flying insect, when I saw the blue dragonfly with the yellow-starred tail and pink hat in the rear-view mirror. It was following us home!

I turned around, and for a brief moment, smiled. I still felt awful.

When we got home, my parents went inside. I sat in the car with Ginger for a few moments. I really wanted Mr. Max to be waiting for me at the front door, but I knew he wasn't. Reluctantly I decided to go over to his grave.

I brought Ginger's cage with me. I sat down on the ground in front of the angel statue on top of Mr. Max's grave. Suddenly, the blue dragonfly fly appeared right on top of the statue. I was glad to see her, so I decided to talk.

"I still feel dragged-down about Mr. Max dying. And Ginger could have died, too. Thanks for what you did. Who are you?"

"I'm Mystie. I'm glad you're speaking to me. And I'm glad I could help. You might feel better if you talk about what happened. Why don't you tell Ginger all about it?"

So I told Ginger everything. I told her how mad I had been with my parents, how mad and sad I was at Mr. Max dying, and how my anger caused me forget to take care of her. By the time I was done, I was crying. I had to wipe my tears on my shirt.

"How do you feel now?" said Mystie in a warm voice.

"I feel very sad, but not as angry anymore. I wish Mr. Max didn't have to die, but I'm glad he's buried in our yard."

I looked right at the ground and yelled at the top of my voice, "Oh Mr. Max I miss you so much!"

At that moment, Ginger started squealing and running around her cage.

"Ginger misses him too", said Mystie.

"So what do we do now?" I asked in confusion.

"*You continue to love each other*", said Mystie.

"Continue to love each other? How? I can still love Ginger, she's right here. But Mr. Max is gone! How can I still love him?"

Mystie flew up to look into my face. Her wings were moving so fast that all I could see were her heart shaped eyes, staring into mine.

"You still love Mr. Max inside your heart. That's where all love comes from. Love never changes. Mr. Max will always be a part of your life."

Then Mystie flew on top of Ginger's cage.

"Your anger blocked the flow of your love. You saw what happened because of that."

"I don't want THAT to happen again," I said in a determined voice.

"It doesn't have to. It's up to you. It's okay to be angry. But don't let your anger create more problems. I'm going to tell you something you can say to yourself whenever you feel angry. I call them "heart words," because when you say them, it helps you stay focused on love.

Mystie started flying all around me, around Ginger inside her cage, and around the angel on the grave. She was flying so fast I could barely see her. But I heard her clearly say:

> I won't let anger get in the way
>
> Of the Love I feel inside each day.
>
> My life is mine to choose how to be,
>
> I choose to be Loving, 'cause that's the real me.

As she finished the last word, she suddenly disappeared! I looked around the yard, but she was gone. I took a deep breath, went through Mystie's words in my head, and then put my hand on top of the angel statue.

"I will always love you Mr. Max."

I picked up Ginger's cage and walked to the front door.

CHAPTER EIGHT

PICTURE THIS

I couldn't wait to get up to my room so I could type Mystie's words on my computer, *exactly* the way that she had said them. As I walked up the steps to my room, I looked at the picture of Mr. Max and me on the mantle. I stopped.

"Mom, can I have that picture on the mantle, the one with Mr. Max and me? I want to put it in my room."

My mom went over to the mantle, picked up the picture and carried it to me. As she handed it over, I saw tears in her eyes. I understood she was missing Mr. Max too. She was grieving in her own way.

"You can still see it every day, mom. It's just in a different place. This picture reminds me of how much Mr. Max loved me.

"Mr. Max did love you so much Jake. Your dad and I are sorry about what happened. Maybe we should have included you."

"It's okay. I just want Mr. Max to know how much I loved...still love him."

With the picture in one hand and Ginger's cage in the other, I went to my room. I put Ginger's cage where it belonged. She started making happy noises. I put the picture on my desk, and started typing on my computer:

I won't let anger get in the way
Of the Love I feel inside each day.
My life is mine to choose how to be,
I choose to be Loving, 'cause that's the real me!

I said the words aloud a few times and I felt better. I thought about what Mystie said. I will never stop loving Mr. Max!

I took out a piece of paper, and started drawing a picture of Mystie. I wanted to remember what she looked like. She's a great friend to my whole family. As I was drawing and looking at the picture on my desk, I was thinking:

Mr. Max was the best cat in the world.

He shared his love with me each day.

He still loves me, and I love him.

Period.

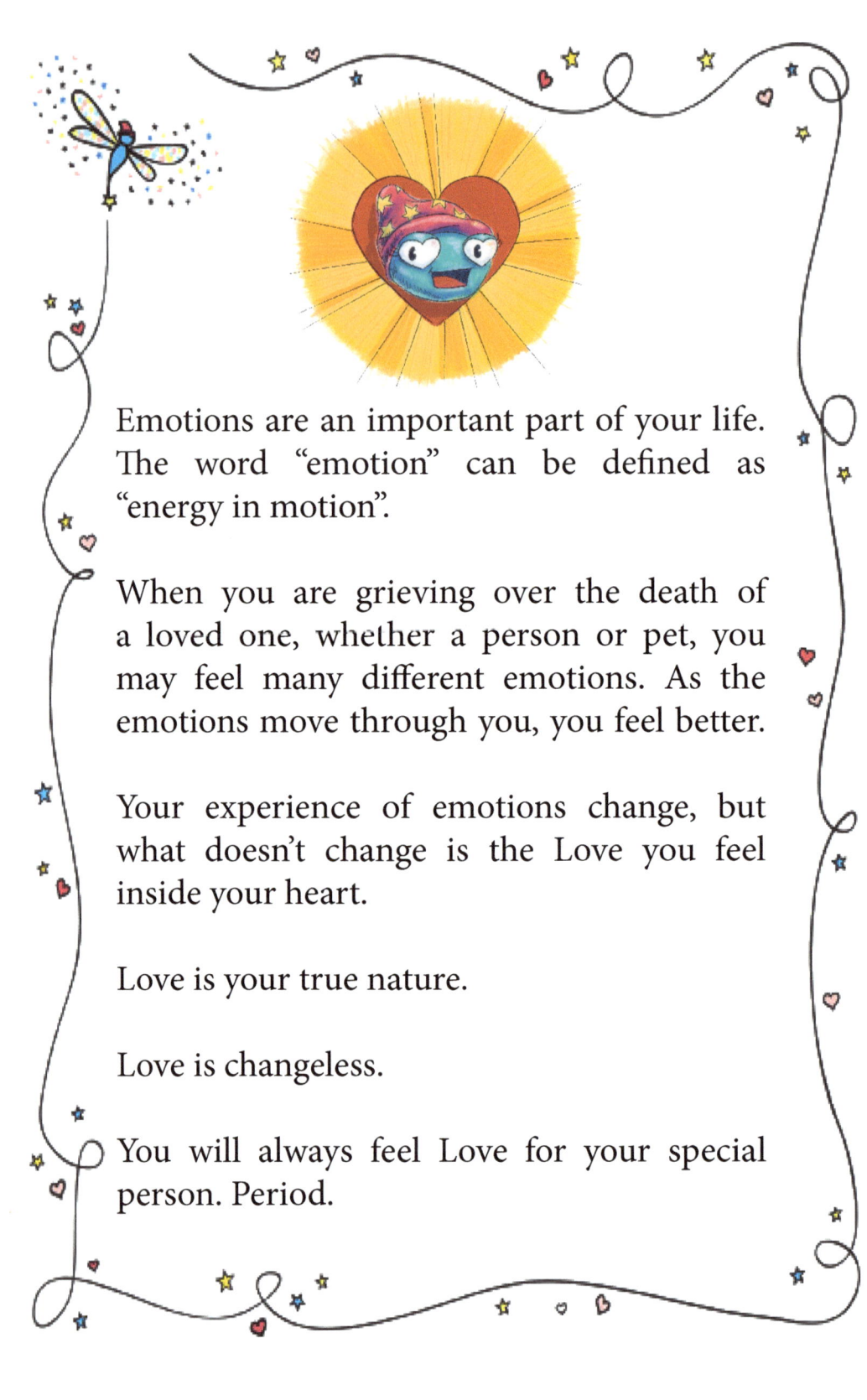

Emotions are an important part of your life. The word "emotion" can be defined as "energy in motion".

When you are grieving over the death of a loved one, whether a person or pet, you may feel many different emotions. As the emotions move through you, you feel better.

Your experience of emotions change, but what doesn't change is the Love you feel inside your heart.

Love is your true nature.

Love is changeless.

You will always feel Love for your special person. Period.

THE QUESTIONS BELOW CAN BE USED TO OPEN A HEALING DIALOGUE WITH A BEREAVED CHILD.

Discussion Questions

1. The words below describe many of the emotions Jake felt throughout the story :

    very sad angry curious excited confused happy mad worried scared upset depressed peaceful anxious

    Have you felt any of these emotions since the death of your loved one?

2. Look at the list again. Can you tell when in the story Jake felt each one? For example, when did Jake feel very sad? When did Jake feel angry? Feel curious ?

3. When do you feel any of those emotions?

4. What emotion became "stuck" inside of Jake?

5. What did Jake forget to do because of his "stuck" emotion?

6. How did Mystie help Jake?

7. How will Jake help himself the next time he feels the emotion of anger?

8. What can you do to help yourself the next time you feel angry?

www.ingramcontent.com/pod-product-compliance
Lightning Source LLC
Chambersburg PA
CBHW041813040426
42450CB00001B/20